GW00738189

First published by Zidane Press

Copyright by Fiona Ledger 2006
Illustrations by Claire Softley Em

Design by Anastasia Sichkarenko

Distributed by:
Turnaround Publisher Services Ltd.
Unit 3
Olympia Trading Estate
London N2Z 6TZ

T: +44 (0)20 8829 3019

ISBN 0954842154

Fiona Ledger has worked as a designer, fund-raiser and free-lance
writer. Her hobbies are art, Englishness and joie de vivre.

Anastasia Sichkarenko, **Claire Softley** and **Emily Atkins** are free-
lance designers and illustrators.

FIONA'S VERY LARGE HANDBOOK OF ENGLISHNESS

POCKET HEDGEHOGS

THE ENGLISH ARE A FUNNY
BUNCH
ALL CHARM AND MANNERS AND
TEA
BUT CROSS THEM IN THEIR
LITTLE GAMES
AND THEY'LL CRUSH YOU LIKE A
FLEA.

THEY'RE ALL UPPER CASE AND
PRONUNCIATION
AND CROQUET ON THE LAWN
BUT WHETHER UPPER OR
LOWER, THEY KNOW
JUST WHERE THEY, AND YOU,
WERE BORN.

THEY RULED THE SEAS, AND
RAN THE WORLD
AND PAINTED THE EMPIRE PINK
BUT LANGUAGE DOES NOT CON-
QUER PEOPLE
IT'S THE VIOLENCE THAT MAKES
YOU THINK.

SHERLOCK GARDENS.

ENGLISHNESS

The question of whom, or what, the English are has puzzled many people for a long time, particularly the English. One shouldn't really mention this fact though, as it may be rude, which the English don't like, but there really is a question about what is Englishness.

Every nation has it's stereotypes, the English have mono-types, which are really just quiet clichés.

We also had a very civil, civil war and then everyone agreed to be polite again and put the monarchy back together (an Orange monarch who became sort of English but with lots of German cousins).

An empire is an immense egotism.
Ralph Waldo Emerson

So apart from the Magna Carta, the British Empire, Cricket, Football, Queen Victoria, hunting, shooting and fishing, the industrial revolution, electricity, warm beer and fish and chips and spam. What have the English ever done for us?

English life, while very pleasant, is rather
bland. I expected kindness and gentility
and I found it, but there is
such a thing as too much couth.
S. J. Perelman

Always remember that you are an
Englishman and therefore have drawn
first prize in the lottery of life.
Cecil Rhodes

OTHER NATIONS USE FORCE, WE
BRITONS ALONE USE MIGHT.
EVELYN WAUGH

Let us pause to consider the English;
Who when they pause to consider themselves they get all reticently thrilled and
tinglish, because every Englishmen is con-
vinced of one thing, that to be an Englishman is to belong to the most exclusive
club there is.
Ogden Nash

The word Chivalry is derived from the French cheval, a horse.
Thomas Bulfinch

Believe it or not, the English and the French use almost exactly the same adjectives to describe each other - bar the word 'insular'," Mr Coldong said. "So the feelings are mutual."
Henry Samuel.

It was Napoleon who described the English 'as a nation of shopkeepers' which did not go down very well. Basically we always hated each other.

To understand Europe, you have to be a
genius - or French.
Madeleine Albright

**iF THE FRENCH WERE REALLY IN-
TELLIGENT, THEY'D SPEAK ENGLISH
WiLFRED SHEED.**

Boy, those French: They have a different
word for everything!"
Steve Martin.

Mad dogs and Englishmen go out in the midday sun. Perhaps this explains why the British bulldog is ugly, incontinent and generally smelly. Perhaps this also explains why drunken Englishmen chase small wild animals on horseback accompanied by large packs of baying dogs and call it a national pastime.

But it was Tobias Smollett in 1762 who felt that things were slightly awry when he commented:
I think for my part one half of the nation is mad – and the other not very sound.

May I ask you what you were hoping to see out of a Torquay bedroom window? Sydney Opera House, perhaps? The Hanging Gardens of Babylon? Herds of wildbeest sweeping majestically by?
Basil Fawlty

Great Britain has lost an Empire and has not yet found a role.
Dean Acheson

The people of England are never so happy as when you tell them they are ruined.
Arthur Murray, The Upholsterer, 1758

HE IS A TYPICAL ENGLISHMAN, AL-WAYS DULL AND USUALLY VIOLENT.
OSCAR WILDE

You never find an Englishman among the Under-dogs-except in England, of course.
Evelyn Waugh

There's nothing the British like better than a bloke who comes from nowhere, makes it, and then gets clobbered.
Melvyn Bragg

IT IS NOT THAT THE ENGLISH-
MAN CAN'T FEEL- IT IS THAT HE
IS AFRAID TO FEEL. HE HAS BEEN
TAUGHT AT HIS PUBLIC SCHOOL
THAT FEELING IS BAD FORM. HE
MUST NOT EXPRESS GREAT JOY
OR SORROW, OR EVEN OPEN HIS
MOUTH TOO WIDE WHEN HE
TALKS - HIS PIPE MIGHT FALL
OUT IF HE DID
E. M. FORSTER

my dog is dead..

have a cup
of tea.

Even crushed against his brother in the tube, the average Englishman pretends desperately he is alone.
Germaine Greer

There is a marvelous turn and trick to British arrogance; its apparent unconsciousness makes it twice as effectual
Catherine Drinker Bowen

The English never smash in a face. They merely refrain from asking it to dinner.
Margaret Halsey

THE ENGLISH ARE BEST EXPLAINED IN TERMS OF TEA, ROAST BEEF AND RAIN. A PERSON IS FIRST WHAT HE EATS, DRINKS AND GETS PELTED WITH.
PIERRE DANINOS

Think of what our Nation stands for,
Books from Boots' and country lanes,
Free speech, free passes, class distinction,
Democracy and proper drains....
John Betjemen .

The British do not expect happiness. I had
the impression, all the time that I lived
there, that they do not want to be happy;
they want to be right.
Quentin Crisp

It was always yet the trick of our English
nation, if they have a good thing, to make it
too common.
William Shakespeare

RELIGION, BRITISH STYLE

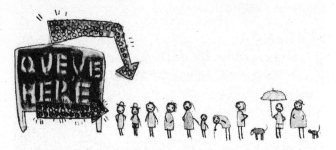

Religion in modern England has mostly been of a wishy-washy kind, ever since Henry VIII's dissolution of the monasteries and the kicking out of the Holy Roman papists. In an uncharacteristic mode he killed quite a lot of people and then set up the Church of England. From then on it was mostly moderate religion of a pragmatic kind that everyone could agree with, and those who didn't went and started America.

The rest went and bothered the colonials in what we called The Empire. Missionaries claimed that there was only one position in religion, which was with the White man on the top.

Poor Uncle Harry
Having become a missionary
Found the natives' morals rather crude.
He and Aunt Mary
Quickly imposed an arbitrary
Ban upon them shopping in the nude.
They all considered this silly and they didn't take it well,
They burnt his boots and several suits and wrecked the Mission Hotel,
They also burnt his mackintosh, which made a disgusting smell....
Uncle Harry's not a missionary now.
Noel Coward

The words of the hymn 'And did those feet in ancient time walk in England's Mountain green...' still continue to be sung in churches up and down the country.

As for the british churchman, he goes to church as he goes to the bathroom, with the minimum of fuss and with no explanation if he can help it.
Ronald Blythe

A consumer's Guide to Religion – The Best Buy – Church of England. It's a jolly friendly faith. If you are one, there's no onus to make everyone else join.
In fact no one need ever know.
Robert Gillespie.

- ARE YOU RELIGIOUS?
- NO, I'M CHURCH OF ENGLAND
ANDY HAMILTON

Foster: I'm still a bit hazy about the Trinity, sir.
Schoolmaster: Three in one, one in three, perfectly straightforward. Any doubts about that see your maths master.
Alan Bennet

Bernard always had a few prayers in the hall and some whiskey afterwards as he was rather pious but Mr Salteena was not very addicted to prayers so he marched up to bed.
Daisy Ashford

In 1980 British church membership stood at 13.4%. Compared to 31% in 1920, this shows a significant decline in church attendance. In 2006 the only two groups who go to Church are the Catholics and the criminals who go to steal the lead off the roof. Occasionally people get married in church but it usually doesn't last.

People in Britain love their old churches, and love the idea of church, they just don't actually want to go and worship in them. The new religion in Britain is home-based, it's based around the fact that the value of your home keeps going up, so you worship it.

Give a man a fish, and you'll feed him for a day. Give him a religion, and he'll starve to death while praying for fish.
Timothy Jones

My church accepts all denominations –
fivers, tenners, twenties
Patrick O'Connell

Heaven is an English policeman, a French cook, a German engineer, an Italian lover and everything organised by the Swiss. Hell is an English cook, a French engineer, a German policeman, a Swiss lover and everything organised by the Italians.
John Elliot

OF COURSE i BELIEVE iN LiFE AFTER DEATH. i'M iN SHOW BUSINESS. i SEE iT HAPPEN ALL THE TIME.
DALE WINTON

I have never been molested when traveling alone on trains. I just have to say a few words and I am immediately left alone: 'Are you a born-again Christian?'
Rita Rudner

If you go into the woods today

If there is such a thing as reincarnation, knowing my luck I'll come back as me.
Rodney Trotter

The only thing father always gave up for
Lent was going to church
Clarence Day

A religious group came to the door yester-
day selling cosmetics. They call themselves
Jojobas's Witnesses
Jeannie Dietz

When it comes to gay priests, even the tab-
loids suddenly find they have a religious
affairs correspondent.
David Hare

THE BEST PRAYER i EVER HEARD
WAS, 'DEAR LORD, PLEASE MAKE
THE KIND OF PERSON MY DOG
THINKS i AM'.
REV. WARREN J. KEATING

Can bishops only move diagonally?
Lester Wood

Baptists are only funny underwater.
Neil Simon

POLITICS.

English politics have mostly consisted of various upper-class twerps invading foreign countries, messing it up and blaming everyone else. In the twentieth century this changed so that middle-class people invaded other countries, messed it up and blamed the upper-classes. In the 21st century the chavs invaded the rest of the world and messed it up, but they were so drunk they didn't notice. Apart from that most English politics is fairly polite.

Politics is derived from two words – poly, meaning many, and tics, meaning small blood-sucking insects.
Chris Clayton

The most interesting things in English politics are the sex scandals and the self-glorification of English prime ministers, unfortunately the two rarely combine. Apart from Churchill and Lloyd-George most English prime ministers have been boring, apart from Margeret Thatcher, who was barking mad. She closed every coal mine in the country because Arthur Scargill was rude about her, destroyed most of British manufacturing, sacked anybody she didn't like and then cried when the Tory party got rid of her. This made her a great Prime Minister, unlike that grey bloke who followed her, John Minor or somebody like that. It's not clear who is prime minister at the moment and nobody cares.

Politics has always been the art of the possible, or if not possible than passable, and failing that you simply make everything presentable.
Henry O'Donnell.

I was allowed to ring the bell for five minutes until everyone was in assembly. It was
the beginning of power.
Jeffrey Archer

Jeffrey Archer, is there no beginning to
your talents?
Clive Anderson

never trust an archer

We find no spectacle so ridiculous as the British public in one of its periodical fits of morality
Lord Macauley

My friends, as I have discovered myself, there are no disasters, only opportunities. And, indeed, opportunities for fresh disasters.
Boris johnson

There's nothing so improves the mood of the party as the imminent execution of a senior colleague.
Alan Clarke

We were all totally shocked when the sexual bombshell was dropped by the former MP, Edwina Curry who confessed to having had an affair with the former PM, John Major. It was all the more irritating that it was the very man who had campaigned on a puritanical 'back to basics' slogan. It was Lady Archer who put it succinctly when she said, 'I am a little surprised, not at Mrs Curry's indiscretion but at a temporary lapse in John Major's taste'.

-SHRED THAT DOCUMENT! NO ONE MUST EVER BE ABLE TO FIND IT AGAIN!
-IN THAT CASE, MINISTER, I THINK IT'S BEST THAT I FILE IT.
JIM HACKER AND BERNARD WOOLLEY, YES MINISTER

Working in Westminster is like having the nutters on the bus beside you every day.
Amanda Platell

Many journalists have fallen for the con-
spiracy theory of government.
They would produce more accurate work if
they adhered to the cock-up theory.
Bernard Ingham

-THE TROUBLE WITH ENGLAND IS
IT'S BEING GOVERNED BY CUNTS.
-QUITE FRANKLY, OLD MAN,
THERE'RE AN AWFUL LOT OF
CUNTS IN ENGLAND, AND THEY DE-
SERVE REPRESENTATION.
REX HARRISON AND UNNAMED MP

I've decided to take up a life of crime, but I
can't decide which political party to join.
Ronnie Kray

If voting changed anything, they'd
abolish it.
Ken Livingstone

Tony Blair is only Bill Clinton with his zip
done up.
Neil Hamilton

Politics are almost as exciting as war and quite as dangerous. In war, you can only be killed once, but in politics – many times.
Winston Churchill

POLITICIANS ARE PEOPLE WHO, WHEN THEY SEE THE LIGHT AT THE END OF THE TUNNEL, ORDER MORE TUNNEL.
JOHN QUINTON

Generally speaking, politicians are generally speaking.
John Sergeant

I'm offended by political jokes. Too often they get elected.
Will Rogers

Political skill is the ability to foretell what is going to happen tomorrow,
next week, next month and next year. And to have the ability afterwards to explain why it didn't happen.
Winston Churchill

When there is a great cry that something should be done, you can depend on it that something remarkable silly probably will be done.
Tony Benn

iF GOD HAD WANTED US TO VOTE, HE WOULD HAVE GiVEN US CANDi-DATES.
JAY LENO

We started off trying to set up a small anarchist community, but
people wouldn't obey the rules
Alan Bennett

She said, 'What do you think of Marx?' I said, ' I think their pants have dropped off but you can't fault their broccoli.'
Victoria Wood

Margaret Thatcher even dressed to the right.
Patrick Murray

Margaret Thatcher is the sort of woman who wouldn't give you your ball back.
Mike Harding

Margaret Thatcher behaved with all the sensitivity of a sex-starved boa constrictor.
Anonymous MP

ANTi-iNTELLEC-TUALiSM.

iNTELLECTUAL – SOME ONE WHO iS RUDE ABOUT OTHER PEOPLE'S BOOKS.

It is well know that the English are anti-intellectual, this is mostly because many intellectuals appear to be foreign, and particularly French or German.

Reactions to the French revolution sealed this view that ideas were dangerous and English culture, particularly in its 'chav' variation embraces a kind of common-sense that distrusts all thinking.

On the other hand the middle-classes are particularly educated and lovers of literature and poetry, and a bit of philosophy, but theory no.

In the past, the English tried to impose a system wherever they went. They destroyed the nation's culture and one of the by-products of their systemitization was that they destroyed their own folk culture.
Martin Carthy

Always in England if you had the type of brain that was capable of understanding T. S. Eliot's poetry or Kant's logic, you could be sure of finding large numbers of people who would hate you violently
D. J. Taylor

THE ENGLISH MAY NOT LIKE MUSIC, BUT THEY ABSOLUTELY LOVE THE NOISE IT MAKES.
THOMAS BEECHAM

Only in Britain could it be thought a defect to be 'too clever by half.' The probability is that too many people are stupid by three-quarters.
John Major

Of the general inadequacy of intellect in the conduct of life Britain is the most majestic exponent. She is instinctively disliked by such people as French, Persians, Hindus, who are clever by nature, and think that intellect can rule. The Italians strayed down this path and disliked us too. But they, and the Greeks, and the Arabs, have a natural perception of other and greater powers and this, I think, is an affinity that binds us. With the others, with the intellectual, it is not our stupidity, but the fact that we prove it posible to live by non-intellectual standards, which makes us disliked.
Freya Stark

England has the most sordid literary scene I've ever seen. They all meet in the same pub. This guy's writing a foreword for this person. They all have to give radio programs, they have to do all this just in order to scrape by. They're all scratching each other's backs.
William Burroughs

English culture is basically homosexual
in the sense that the men only really
care about other men
Germaine Greer

In England, at any rate, education produces
no effect whatsoever. If it did, it would
prove a serious danger to the upper classes,
and probably lead to acts of violence in
Grosvenor Square.
Oscar Wilde

In my day, the principal concerns of university students were sex, smoking dope, riot-
ing and learning. Learning was something
you did only when the first three weren't
available.
Bill Bryson

Most people tire of a lecture in ten minutes;
clever people can do it in five. Sensible
people never go to lectures at all.
Stephen Leacock

An intellectual is someone who has found
something more interesting than sex.
Edgar Wallace

There's nothing as stupid as an educated
man, if you can get him off the thing he
was educated in.
Will Rogers

If one would only teach the English how to talk, and the Irish how to listen, society here would be quite civilised.
Oscar Wilde

I know I've got a degree. Why does that mean I have to spend my life with intellectuals? I've got a life-saving certificate but I don't spend my evenings diving for a rubber brick with my pyjamas on
Victoria Wood

If a man is a fool, you don't train him out of being a fool by sending him to university. You merely turn him into a trained fool, ten times more dangerous.
Desmond Bagley

iT'S MONA LiSA WHO'S SYMMETRi-CAL, iNNiT?'
JADE GOODY

They were trying to use me as an escape goat.
Jade Goody

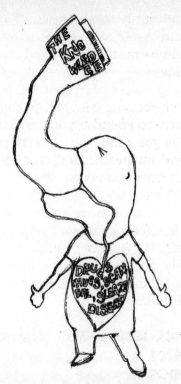

I HAVE BEEN DESCRIBED AS A
LIGHTHOUSE IN THE MIDDLE OF THE
BOG: BRILLIANT BUT USELESS.
CONNOR CRUISE O'BRIEN

SPORTS

Practically every game played international-
ly today was invented in Britain, and when
foreigners became good enough to match or
even defeat the British, the British quickly
invented a new game.
Peter Ustinov

I'm afraid I play no outdoor games at all,
except dominoes. I have sometimes
played dominoes outside a French cafe.
Oscar Wilde

Serious sport is war minus the shooting
George Orwell

WHAT ON EARTH HAS THIS SYN-
CHRONISED SWIMMING GOT TO
DO WITH ANYTHING? LET ALONE
SPORT?
FRANK KEATING

'Apart from the goals, Norway haven't scored'
Terry Venables

'HE DRIBBLES A LOT AND THE OPPOSITION DON'T LIKE IT: YOU CAN SEE IT ALL OVER THEIR FACES'
RON ATKINSON

If you'd given me the choice of beating four men and smashing in a goal from 30 yards against Liverpool or going to bed with Miss World, it would have been a difficult choice. Luckily I had both. It's just that you do one of those things in front of 50,000 people.
George Best

'When the seagulls follow the trawler, it's because they think that sardines will be thrown into the sea'
Eric Cantona

Winning doesn't matter as long as you win
Vinny Jones

I tend to believe that cricket is the greatest
thing that God ever created on earth...
certainly greater than sex although
sex isn't too bad either. But everyone
knows which comes first when it's a
question of cricket or sex.
Harold Pinter

Many continentals think life is a game; the
English think cricket is a game
George Mikes

Cricket – a game which the English, not being a spiritual people, have
invented in order to give themselves some
conception of eternity.
Lord Mancroft

I only wish some of the player's
trousers fitted better.
Prince Philip, Duke of Edinburgh

Gary Lineker: So Gordon, if you were English, what formation would you play?

Gordon Strachan: If I was English I'd top myself!

Pundit Strachan shows why the BBC hired him for Euro 2004

WHEN MIDDLE-CLASS PEOPLE AND WOMEN STARTED GOING TO MATCHES, i THOUGHT iT'S A SHAME THAT HOOLIGANISM HAS STOPPED BECAUSE THAT USED TO KEEP THEM OUT.
FRANK SKINNER

The FA has given me a pat on the back. I've taken violence off the terracing and onto the pitch. Vinny Jones, referring in 1991 to the many suspensions imposed on him throughout his career

'These are the boys, their balls between their legs'
Amanda Redington GMTV

There are really three things to learn in skiing: how to put on your skis, how to slide downhill and how to walk along the hospital corridor.
Lord Mancroft

Modern football shirts look like the work of a chimpanzee on drugs let loose at Brentford Nylons
Andrew Shields

'HER LEGS WERE KEPT TIGHTLY TOGETHER: SHE'S GIVING NOTHING AWAY'
GYMNASTICS COMMENTATOR BBC

If Everton were playing down at the bottom of my garden, I'd draw the curtains.
Bill Shankly

I had lunch with a chess champion the
other day. I knew he was chess champion
because it took him 20 minutes to pass the
salt.
Eric Sykes

Fishing is a jerk on one end of the line wait-
ing for a jerk on the other end of the line.
Michael Palin

The advantage of the rain is, that if you
have a quick bike, there's no advantage
Barry Sheene

I cannot see for the life of me why the um-
pires, the only two people on a cricket field
who are not going to get grass stains on
their knees are the only 2 people allowed to
wear dark trousers
Katherine Whitehorn

Serena Williams looks forward to
'Wimbledon' – the movie which depicts a
plucky Briton coming from nowhere
to win the tournament

Cricket is basically baseball on Valium
Robin Williams

Don't forget jeans are not allowed on match
days or away trips. And if you're going to
get pissed or poke a girl, do it before
midnight.
Mike Gatting

New Yorkers love it when you spill
your guts out there. Spill your guts at
Wimbledon and they make you stop and
clean it up.
Jimmy Connors

i DON'T WANT TO SOUND PARA-
NOiD, BUT THAT ELECTRONIC LINE
JUDGE KNOWS WHO i AM
JOHN MCENROE

SEX

If sex wasn't necessary for procreation, then the English would undoubtedly have abolished it. However since it must be done it is mostly done as quickly and quietly as possible, so is not to disturb the neighbors.

IT HAS TO BE ADMITTED THAT WE ENGLISH HAVE SEX ON THE BRAIN, WHICH IS VERY UNSATISFACTORY PLACE TO HAVE IT.
MALCOLM MUGGERIDGE

Sex has never been an obsession with me. It's just like eating a bag of crisps. Quite nice, but nothing marvellous.
Boy George

Too much sex on the television will eventually break the stand.

CONTINENTAL PEOPLE HAVE SEX LIVES- THE ENGLISH HAVE HOT-WATER BOTTLES.
GEORGE MIKES

In the old days a lot of people, men as well as women, didn't quite know what to expect from sex so they didn't worry when it didn't work out too well.
Kingsley Amis

Sex and taxes are in many ways the same. Tax does to cash what sex makes to genes. It dispenses assets among the population as a whole. Sex, not death, is the great leveller.
Steve Jones

For flavour, instant sex will never supersede the stuff you have to peel and cook.
Quentin Crisp

Now that the whole dizzying and delirious range of sexual possibilities has been boiled down to that one big, boring, bulimic word. RELATIONSHIP.
Julie Burchill

AN EMPTY ALUMINIUM CIGAR TUBE FILLED WITH ANGRY WASPS MAKES AN INEXPENSIVE VIBRATOR.
TOP TIP, VIZ

All my mother told me about sex was that the man goes on top, and the woman goes on the bottom. For three years my husband and I slept in bunk beds.
Joan Rivers

People think I hate sex. I don't. I just don't like things that stop you seeing the television properly.
Victoria Wood

Told to Laurence Oliver's 5 year old daughter Tamsin, when she asked what 2 dogs were doing together.
The doggie in front has suddenly gone blind, and the other one has very kindly offered to push him all the way to St Dunstan's
Noel Coward

Sex is one of the nine reasons for reincarnation. The other eight are unimportant.
Henry Miller

Even though there is no question that sex is a nicer activity than watching football (no nil-nil draws, no offside trap, no cup upsets, and you're warm), in the normal run of things, the feelings it engenders are simply not as intense as those brought about by a one-in-a-lifetime last-minute Championship winner.
Nick Hornby

THE WOMAN i BROKE UP WiTH iS GOiNG ROUND TELLiNG ALL HER FRiENDS THAT i GAVE HER AN ANTiCLiMAX.
RiCHARD LEWiS

I have no problem with British men. I think there is something endearing about desperation and hopelessness.
Melinda Messenger

I'll come to your room at eight o'clock. If I'm late start without me.
Tallulah Bankhead

Sex with Nicholas Soames was like
having a large wardrobe fall on top of
you with the key still in the lock.
Anon

**THE ONLY PLACE MEN WANT
DEPTH IN A WOMAN IS IN HER
DECOLLETAGE.
ZSA ZSA GABOR**

To keep a man you must be a maid in the
living room, a cook in the kitchen and a
whore in the bedroom. I hire the other
two and take care of the bedroom bit myself.
Jerry Hall

I am always looking for meaningful one-
night stands.
Dudley Moore

You were born with your legs apart. They'll
send you to the grave in a Y-shaped coffin.
Joe Orton

i ONCE MADE LOVE TO A FEMALE CLOWN. SHE TWISTED MY PENIS INTO A POODLE.
DAN WHITNEY

I don't know what I am, darling. I've tried several varieties of sex. The conventional position makes me claustrophobic. And the others give me either a stiff neck or lockjaw.
Tallulah Bankhead

They guy dumped me because he said I have low self-esteem. I said, 'No kidding. I slept with you didn't I?'
Tracey Macdonald

It doesn't matter what you do in the bedroom as long as you don't do it in the street and frighten the horses.
Mrs Patrick Campbell

THE COLD OF THE POLAR REGIONS WAS NOTHING TO THE CHILL OF AN ENGLISH BEDROOM.
FRIDTJOF NANSEN

I was mistaken for a prostitute once in the last war. When a GI asked me what I charged, I said, 'Well, dear, what do your mother and sisters normally ask for?'
Thora Hird

ALL THIS FUSS ABOUT SLEEPING TOGETHER. FOR PHYSICAL PLEASURE i'D SOONER GO TO THE DENTIST ANY DAY.
EVELYN WAUGH

As I grow older and older and totter towards the tomb, I find that I care less and less who goes to bed with whom.
Dorothy L. Sayers

Now that I'm 78, I do tantric sex because it's very slow. My favourite position is called the plumber. You stay in all day but nobody comes.
John Mortimer

I'm not into that one-night thing. I think a person should get to know someone and even be in love with them before you use them and degrade them.
Steve Martin

If it's true that men only prefer watching football to having sex because football lasts longer, then the answer lies in their own hands.
Mary Riddell

In my day I would only have sex with a man if I found him extremely attractive. These days, girls seem to choose them in much the same way as they might choose to suck on a boiled sweet.
Mary Wesley

At the age of ninety-seven, Blake was asked at what age the sex drive goes: 'You'll have to ask somebody older than me'.
Eubie Blake

MANNERS AND ETIQUETTE

It is impossible for en Englishman to open
his mouth without making some other Englishman hate or despite him
George Bernard Shaw

Nothing more rapidly inclines a person to
go into a monastery than reading a book on
etiquette. There are so many trivial ways
which it is possible to commit some social
sin.
Quentin Crisp

**MANNERS ARE ESPECIALLY THE
NEED OF THE PLAIN. THE PRETTY
CAN GET AWAY WITH ANYTHING.
EVELYN WAUGH**

Curtsey while you're thinking what
to say. It saves time.
Lewis Carroll

We don't bother much about dress and manners in England, because as a nation we don't dress well and we've no manners.
George Bernard Shaw

I tried to keep in mind the essential rules of British conduct which the major had carefully instilled in me:
1. The English never speak to anyone unless they have been properly introduced (except in case of shipwreck).
2. You must never talk about God or your stomach
Pierre Daninos

BOY GEORGE iS ALL ENGLAND NEEDS – ANOTHER QUEEN WHO CAN'T DRESS
JOAN RIVERS

The trouble nowadays is that no one stares, however outrageous one's behaviour.
Quentin Crisp

The English like eccentrics. They just
don't like them living next door.
Julian Clary

The English are polite at telling lies, the
Americans are polite by telling the truth.
Malcolm Bradbury

To Americans, English manners are far
more frightening than none at all.
Randall Jarrell

IF AN ENGLISHMAN GETS RUN
DOWN BY A TRUCK HE APOLOGIZ-
ES TO THE TRUCK.
JACKIE MASON

On the Continent people have good
food; in England people have good
table manners.
George Mikes

Comedies of manners swiftly become obsolete when there are no longer any manners.
Noel Coward

AN ENGLISHMAN, EVEN IF HE IS ALONE, FORMS AN ORDERLY QUEUE OF ONE.
GEORGE MIKES

Beware the conversationalist who adds 'in conclusion'. He is merely starting afresh.
Robert Morley

Taboo areas of conversation: the toupees worn by our friends; not having any credit cards; a fear of ladybirds; being unable to admit that you have gone right off what everyone thinks is your favorite dish; never having tried marijuana; the admission that one does not have a satisfactory sex life; the admission that one does not even particularly want a satisfactory sex life.
Miles Kington

When a man opens a car door for his wife, it's either a new car or a new wife.
Prince Philip

Women are never disarmed by compliments. Men always are. That is the difference between the two sexes.
Oscar Wilde

WHAT ALWAYS STAGGERS ME IS THAT WHEN PEOPLE BLOW THEIR NOSES, THEY ALWAYS LOOK INTO THEIR HANKIES TO SEE WHAT CAME OUT. WHAT DO THEY EXPECT TO FIND? A SILVER SIXPENCE?
BILLY CONNOLLY

It was a delightful visit; perfect, in being much too short.
Jane Austen

We really like dowdiness in England. It's absolutely incurable in us, I believe.
Peter Shaffer

An English football hooligan, answering charges in court declared; If we were doing this in the Falklands they would love it. It's part of our heritage. The British have always been fighting wars.

As a nation we are unfortunately well known for hooliganism. The Dowager Marchioness of Reading responded to the latest outbreak of violence involving England supporters by saying;
Now that we don't have a war, what's wrong with a good punch-up? We are a nation of yobs. Without that characteristic, how did we colonise the world? I don't agree with broken glass and knives. But what an English guy does is fight with his fists; a good clean fight....

The etiquette question that troubles so many fastidious people on New Year's Day is: How am I ever going to face those people again?
Judith Martin

VULGARITY IS SIMPLY THE
CONDUCT OF OTHER PEOPLE.
OSCAR WILDE

LIFESTYLE, HOBBIES AND PLEASURE.

Actually being English is a hobby that becomes obsessive, particularly as it has no intrinsic meaning.
John Smith.

Sunday is the day God took off from creating the world to take Mrs. God around IKEA
Jeff Green

Activities outside the home include a great deal of retail therapy amongst young and old which seems to have become a national obsession.

Morris Dancing –This is very much an expression of our English cultural identity.

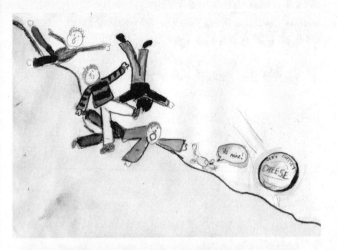

CHEESE ROLLING ON COOPER'S HILL, GLOUCESTERSHIRE WHERE THOUSANDS OF SPECTATORS CONGREGATE TO WATCH THE TRADITIONAL 7lB DOUBLE GLOUCESTER CHEESE HURTLE DOWN A STEEP SLOPE, PURSUED BY DOZENS OF RUNNING, ROLLING COMPETITORS, THE FASTEST OF WHOM WINS THE CHEESE.

The natural instinct of the English is to keep to themselves. That is why they leave their homes and congregate in clubs. A club is a place where a few hundred Englishmen can be alone. The best literary, legal and political brains in the country assemble, sit down and remain silent on the burning questions of the day.
George Mikes

-Bubble, what do you do?
- I don't know. Get paid.
Edina Monsoon and Bubble, Absolutely Fabulous

A FOOLPROOF PLAN FOR NOT GETTING A JOB – SHOW UP FOR YOUR INTERVIEW WEARING FLIP-FLOPS.
ALAN DAVIES

The trouble with unemployment is that the minute you wake up in the morning, you're on the job.
Slappy White

When you go to work, if your name is on the building, you're rich. If your name is on your desk, you're middle class. And if your name is on your shirt, you're poor.
Rich Hall

Not everyone works in an office, including those who work in an office.
Jim Davidson

HOLIDAY & PLEASURE

We sat on the front (at Deal) and watched the hardy English children and a few adults advancing, mauve with cold, into the cheerless waves.
Noel Coward

Somebody said to me this morning, 'to what do you attribute your longevity?' I don't know. I mean, I couldn't have planned my life out better. By all accounts I should be dead! The abuse I put my body though: the drugs, the alcohol, the lifestyle I've lived the last 30 years!
Ozzy Osbourne

Lying in bed would be an altogether perfect and supreme experience if only one had a coloured pencil long enough to draw on the ceiling.
G.K. Chesterton

People seem to enjoy things more when they know a lot of other people have been left out of the pleasure.
Russell Baker

A cigarette is the perfect type of perfect pleasure. It is exquisite and leaves one quite unsatisfied. What more can one want?
Oscar Wilde

It is impossible to enjoy idling thoroughly
unless one has plenty of work to do.
Jerome. K. Jerome.

Why pay the earth for expensive jigsaws?
Just take a bag of frozen chips from the
freezer and try piecing together potatoes.
Top tip, Viz

SHOPPING

PEOPLE WHO SAY MONEY CAN'T BUY YOU HAPPINESS JUST DON'T KNOW WHERE TO SHOP.
TARA PALMER - TOMKINSON

I love to shop after a bad relationship. I buy a new outfit and it makes me feel better. Sometimes when I see a really great outfit, I'll break up with someone on purpose.
Rita Rudner

Like all antique shops it was dingy outside and dark and smelly within. I don't know why it is, but the proprietors of these establishments always seem to be cooking some sort of stew in the back room.
P.G. Wodehouse

My son is always buying me things, but I never let him buy me furniture.
Sheila, mother of Elton John

Some things to read if you want to take it further

Ackroyd, Peter *Albion: The Origins of the English Imagination* (2002)

Barnes, Julian *England England* (1999)

Bracewell, Michael *England is Mine: Pop Culture in Albion. From Wilde to Goldie* (1998)

Bragg, Billy *The Progressive Patriot* (2006)

Clifford, Sue & King, Angela *England in Particular: A Celebration of the Commonplace, the Local, the Vernacular & the Distinctive* (2006)

Fox, Kate *Watching the English: The Hidden Rules of English Behaviour* (2004)

Gervais, David Literary Englands: *Versions of Englishness in Modern Writing* (1993)

Kumar, Krishan *The Making of English National Identity* (2003)

Langford, Paul *Englishness Identified: Manners and Character 1650 – 1850* (2000)

Mikes, George *How to be a Brit* (1986)

Orwell, George *England your England* (First Published 1941), *The Lion and the Unicorn* (1941)

Paxman, Jeremy *The English: A Portrait of a People* (1999)

Roger Scruton *England: An elegy* (2001)

Smith, Godfrey *The English Companion: An Idiosyncratic A – Z of England and Englishness* (1996)

Webster, Wendy *Englishness and Empire 1939 – 1965* (2005)

Winn, Christopher *I never knew that about England* (2005)